TRUE OR FALSE?

It's impossible to tell what the owner of this skull looked like. He or she has been dead too long!

FALSE!

Your skull carries a lot of information about your face. Forensic artists know how to "read" that information. They use a skull to draw or sculpt a person's face. And when police need to identify burned or rotted bodies, a forensic artist comes in handy.

And that's not all they can do. Read on to find out how art can solve crimes.

Book design Red Herring Design/NYC

Library of Congress Cataloging-in-Publication Data
Denega, Danielle.
Have you seen this face? : the work of forensic artists / by Danielle Denega.
p. cm. — (24/7 : science behind the scenes)
Includes bibliographical references and index.
ISBN-13: 978-0-531-11823-8 (lib. bdg.)   978-0-531-15458-8 (pbk.)
ISBN-10: 0-531-11823-1 (lib. bdg.)   0-531-15458-0 (pbk.)
1. Police artists. 2. Criminals—Identification. 3. Composite
drawing. 4. Facial reconstruction (Anthropology) I. Title.
HV8073.4.D46 2007
363.25'8—dc22   2006020870

HAVE YOU SEEN THIS FACE?

The Work of Forensic Artists

Danielle Denega

WARNING: All of the cases described in this book are real. One involves a skull. A *human* skull, that is. The other two? They involve murder and kidnapping.

Franklin Watts®
A Division of Scholastic Inc.
New York • Toronto • London • Auckland • Sydney
Mexico City • New Delhi • Hong Kong
Danbury, Connecticut

CONTENTS

These cases are 100% real. Find out how forensic artists helped catch some criminals.

A skull is found in Yorktown, NY.

15 Case #1:
The Case of the Skull in the Woods

A skeleton is found, and no one knows who it was! Does the victim's skull hold the key to his identity?

25 Case #2:
The Man Who Knew Too Much

A woman is killed in a park, and her husband lives to tell the story. Can a forensic artist unmask the murderer?

A man describes his wife's killer in Spokane, WA.

35 Case #3:
The Case of the Missing Girl

A four-year-old girl is kidnapped by her mother. Thirteen years later, police are still searching for her. But what does the girl—now 17 years old—look like?

A father looks for his daughter in Washington, DC.

FORENSIC DOWNLOAD

Here's even more amazing stuff about forensic art for you to draw on.

Drawing a person is hard enough when your subject is right there. Forensic artists do better than that.

FORENSIC 411

They draw people they've never seen before. They sketch suspects from eyewitness descriptions. They can look at an old photo and imagine how the person looks today. They can even re-create a face from a skull. Want to find out how they do it?

IN THIS SECTION:

- ▶ how forensic artists and cops really TALK;
- ▶ how an artist puts a FACE TOGETHER;
- ▶ who else works at the CRIME SCENES.

A Picture Is Worth 1,000 Words

Forensic artists—and police officers—have their own way of speaking. Find out what their vocabulary means.

"We need someone on this case who knows **forensic art**. We've got four eyewitnesses, so let's see if we can get a good **composite image**."

forensic art
(fuh-REN-sik art) art that helps solve a crime or is used in a court of law

composite image
(kuhm-POZ-it IH-muj) a type of forensic art in which an artist creates an image of a person based on descriptions of different parts of the face

The word composite means "made up of different parts."

"Believe it or not, we'll be able to **reconstruct** this person's face from that skull."

reconstruct
(REE-khun-strukt) to build again

Say What?

identify
(eye-DEN-tuh-fye)
to establish who
a person is

"All that's left
of the body is
a skull. It's not
going to be easy
to identify the
victim."

features
(FEE-churz) the
parts that make up
the human face

"Send the skull
to the lab. See
if the forensic
artists can figure
out what this
person's features
were like."

**Here's some other
lingo a forensic artist
might use on the job.**

hit
(hit) a successful identification
"Sir, I think we got a **hit** on
that missing girl from a few
years ago."

Jane Doe
(jayn doh) an unidentified
female body
"Look at the shape of the
forehead. It's female. We've got
ourselves a **Jane Doe** here."

John Doe
(jon doh) an unidentified
male body
"Did we get an ID on that
John Doe found in the
woods last week?"

space alien
(spayss AY-lee-uhn) an odd-
looking composite image
"That composite is a **space
alien**. It's not going to help
us identify anyone."

NOSE

overall shape: Is it round, squared, or triangular?
top, or bridge: Is it straight or curved?
tip: Does it curve up or down toward the mouth?

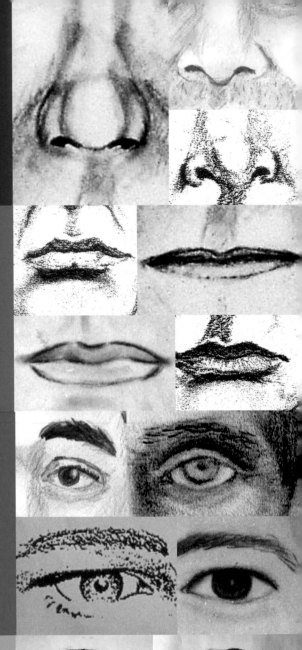

MOUTH

width: Is it narrow, wide, or in between?
lips: Are they thin or thick? Is the top lip the same thickness as the bottom?

EYES

color: Blue? Brown? Green?
eyelids: Are they wide open or partly closed? Is the upper lid visible?
eyebrows: Are they bushy or thin? Straight, highly arched, or in between?

SHAPE

Is the face square or oval? Do the facial features match the size of the face?

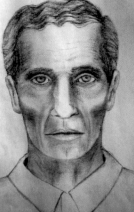

Putting the Pieces Together

A composite artist guides a witness to describe a suspect's face—feature by feature.

A burglar dashes into a jewelry store waving a gun. The store owner hands over some cash. The thief grabs it and runs out. The store owner got a good look at the thief. But how do the police find out what the burglar looks like?

They call a forensic artist. Forensic artists create something called composite images. Composite means "made up of different parts."

Most **witnesses** can't describe a whole face very well. But they can usually remember many of the features if someone asks the right questions.

Forensic artists take witnesses through a **suspect's** face, feature by feature. Then they fit the pieces of the face together into a final image. Check out some of the things they look for on these pages.

The Forensic Team

Forensic artists work as part of a team. Here's a look at some of the experts who help solve crimes.

FORENSIC DNA SPECIALISTS

They collect DNA from body fluids, skin, or hair left at the scene. They use this evidence to identify victims and suspects.

MEDICAL EXAMINERS

They're medical doctors who investigate suspicious deaths. They try to find out when and how someone died. They often direct other members of the team.

FORENSIC DENTISTS

They identify victims and criminals by their teeth or bitemarks.

POLICE DETECTIVES/ AGENTS

They collect evidence, investigate crimes, and arrest suspects.

FORENSIC ARTISTS

They create images of suspects and victims when it's not clear what a person looks like.

FORENSIC ANTHROPOLOGISTS

They're called in to identify victims by studying bones.

FINGERPRINT EXAMINERS

They find, photograph, and collect fingerprints at the scene. Then they compare them to prints they have on record.

TRUE-LIFE CASE FILES!

24 hours a day, 7 days a week, 365 days a year, forensic artists are solving mysteries.

IN THIS SECTION:

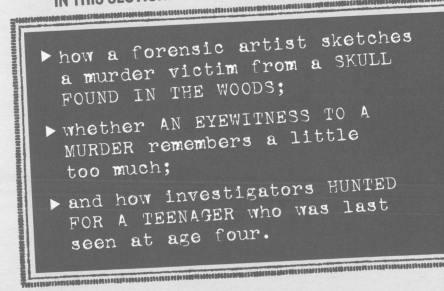

▶ how a forensic artist sketches a murder victim from a SKULL FOUND IN THE WOODS;

▶ whether AN EYEWITNESS TO A MURDER remembers a little too much;

▶ and how investigators HUNTED FOR A TEENAGER who was last seen at age four.

Here's how forensic artists get the job done.

What does it take to draw someone you've never seen? Good forensic artists don't just make guesses. They follow a step-by-step process.

As you read the case studies, you can follow along with their process. Keep an eye out for the icons below. They'll clue you in to each step along the way.

THE QUESTION (?) At the beginning of a case, forensic artists **identify the question** they need to answer.

THE EVIDENCE The next step is to **gather and analyze evidence**. Artists use whatever information they have about their subject. That could be an eyewitness account, an old photo, or a skull.

THE CONCLUSION (!) A finished sculpture or image is a **forensic artist's conclusion**. If the image is accurate, it might lead to the arrest of a suspect or the identification of a victim.

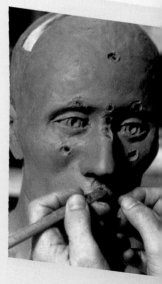

New Croton Reservoir
Yorktown, New York
July 2002

The Case of the Skull in the Woods

A skeleton is found, and no one knows who it was! Does the victim's skull hold the key to his identity?

Body Found!

To solve a mysterious murder, police first need to identify the victim.

Joy Mann, a forensic artist from Illinois, was brought in to help identify the skull.

Police in Westchester County, New York, were stumped. In July 2002, a group of hikers had found a **corpse**. The body had been left in the woods near the New Croton Reservoir in Yorktown. Most of its flesh had rotted away. The **skull** lay in bits and pieces.

Police believed they had a murder on their hands. But they had no idea who had been killed. By fall, they had made no progress. Without knowing the **victim**, how could they catch the murderer?

The investigators needed help. They went all the way to Illinois to find it. They called Joy Mann, a forensic artist with the sheriff's office in Illinois. She also runs her own company, MannHunters Forensic Artists. Mann is an **expert** at **postmortem** images. She re-creates life-like faces from bare bones.

THE QUESTION **(?)** Over the phone, Mann agreed to take the case. Her job: Study the **remains** found near the reservoir. Then answer the question, What did this John Doe look like when he was alive?

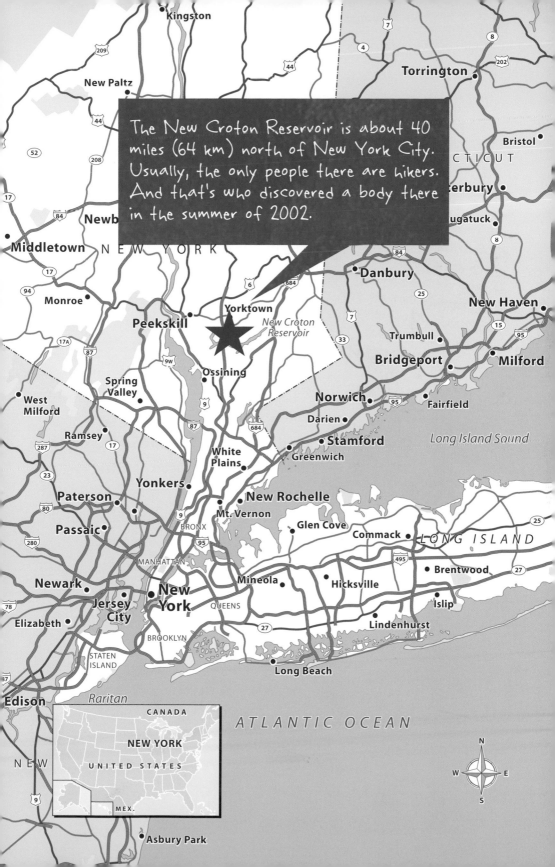

The New Croton Reservoir is about 40 miles (64 km) north of New York City. Usually, the only people there are hikers. And that's who discovered a body there in the summer of 2002.

This is part of a human skull. When Mann received the skull from the New York case, it was in pieces. Her first step was to put the pieces together. Then, she could begin to figure out what the face looked like.

[Heavyweight]
An adult male human head weighs about 8 pounds (3.6 kg).

The Westchester police showed Mann the case file. She studied the **evidence** for any information that might help.

Mann found a report from a **forensic** anthropologist and one from a forensic dentist. They both concluded that the bones came from a Hispanic male. The victim was between 20 and 35 years old.

Crime scene photos came next. Forensic artists look for any hair, clothing, or soft tissue found on the body. Mann noticed a little bit of hair on the skull. It was dark and short. She also noticed a slight overbite in the teeth.

Mann now had a general image of the victim in her mind. It was time for the details. They arrived soon—in a package in the mail. Inside she found exactly what she needed: one human skull—in pieces—and a set of teeth.

Mann unpacked the box and sorted through the pieces. Did she have enough to work with?

THE BARE BONES

Can a forensic artist re-create a face when part of the skull is missing?

Forensic artists often have to work with an incomplete skull. Sometimes that's a problem. Sometimes it's not. It depends which pieces are missing. Some bones are more important to the shape of a face than others.

The top of the skull is called the **cranium**. Sometimes, it has been broken into pieces by a bullet or during an **autopsy**. That's OK. A forensic artist can usually use what's left to figure out the shape of the head.

The bridge of the nose is called the **nasal bone**. Without it, an artist can only guess at the shape of the nose.

Your cheekbones are called the **zygomatic bones**. They play a big role in shaping your face. Without them, a good **reconstruction** is nearly impossible. If one cheekbone exists, an artist can usually use it to re-create the missing cheekbone.

The lower jawbone is called the **mandible**. It is the strongest bone in your face. It holds your lower teeth in place. It often becomes separated from the rest of the skull. In some cases, a forensic artist can re-create a missing mandible. If not, the shape of the jaw is then impossible to guess.

[Face Time]

The 14 bones at the front of your skull hold your eyes in place and form your facial features.

19

Building the Head

Mann turns a box of bones into something that looks like a human being.

With the head in hand, Mann was ready to start. She sorted through the pieces of the skull. All the important pieces were there.

Mann spent several days putting the skull together. She glued the pieces in place and put the teeth where they belonged. The finished skull showed the marks of a violent death. Several teeth were missing.

Next, Mann glued **tissue markers** to the skull. Tissue markers are small, eraser-like pieces of plastic. They show how deep the soft tissue was on various parts of the face. Forensic artists cut them to specific lengths. They place them where flesh once attached to the bone.

How did Mann know where the tissue markers go and how long they should be? That's based on whether the dead person is a male or a female. It's also based on the dead person's ethnic background. People of different genders tend to have different amounts of soft tissue on the

This is the actual skull found by the hikers. The white things sticking out of the skull are tissue markers. Joy Mann glued these tissue markers onto the skull to show how deep the flesh probably was at these places on the face.

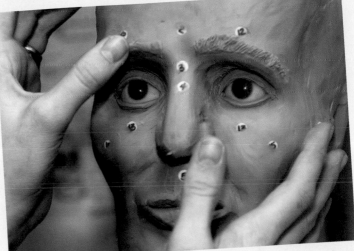

After the tissue markers are in place, some forensic artists create a sculpture of the subject's face. Here, a forensic artist from the Michigan State Police works on a reconstruction of a face on a human skull.

different parts of their faces. So do people of different ethnic groups.

Researchers have created charts for artists to work with. These show the lengths of tissue markers for different categories of people.

Mann had been told by other forensic experts that the victim was a Hispanic male around age 20 to 35. So she checked the chart that matched these details. She added the tissue markers.

At this point, some forensic artists create a **sculpture** of the person's head. They spread clay on the skull. They use the tissue markers to figure out how deep the clay should be on different parts of the face.

But Joy Mann has a different technique.

Drawing the Face

Mann puts pencil to paper, and makes the dead come to life.

This is Joy Mann's sketch of the victim found near the New Croton Reservoir. Mann created this image using only the skull and tissue marker measurements.

The tissue markers were in place on the skull. At this point in the process, Joy Mann always creates a drawing.

For this John Doe, first she took photos of the skull from the front and sides. Then, she placed a piece of tracing paper over the photos. She outlined the face, following the tissue markers. In certain places she was sure of the shape. The jaw and upper cheeks, for instance, follow the outline of the bones. Eyelids, eyebrows, and lips don't follow the bone structure. They required more of a guess.

Mann added the final details. She sketched in hair and eyelashes and ears.

THE CONCLUSION

Her job was done. She had created a drawing of what the victim looked like. But would it help identify the victim? Mann could only wait and see.

Who Was John Doe?

A TV show helps solve the four-month-old mystery.

On November 19, 2002, a TV station broadcast Mann's drawing. Not long after, investigators got a call. A woman told police she was shocked to see the sketch on TV. The drawing looked just like her boyfriend, who had disappeared in July. The man's name was Manuel Delacruz. He was 31 years old. And he was Hispanic.

Delacruz hadn't been seen in four months. One night in July, witnesses saw two people force Delacruz and another man into a car at gunpoint. The other man later escaped from the car.

Police got a **DNA** sample from Delacruz's home. They compared it to DNA from the body found at the reservoir. The two samples matched.

Thanks to the work of Joy Mann, the body had a name. And the story behind the murder had begun to take shape. Manuel Delacruz spent his final hours near the New Croton Reservoir. Police are still investigating Delacruz's murder. They can't release more details about the case. But, for now, at least his friends and family have some answers. 24/7

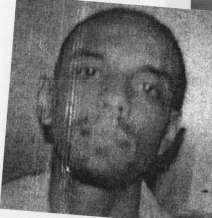

This is a photo of the victim. His name is Manuel Delacruz. Although the sketch wasn't exact, it was close enough for someone who knew Delacruz well—his girlfriend—to recognize him.

Joy Mann discusses putting a face on the dead with postmortem images.

24/7: Why are postmortem images so important?

MANN: It's important to identify the victim in order to go on with an investigation. Many people need to see an image to recognize a person. A description just isn't enough.

24/7: How much guessing do you do when you make a postmortem image?

MANN: The charts showing lengths of tissue markers do not give us information for some parts of the face. These parts include the eyelids, shape of the lips, and possibly the tip of the nose. A forensic artist makes educated guesses about these features. Also, sometimes there is no information about the victim's hair. In that case, it's okay to guess as well.

24/7: What is a common problem you run into when creating a postmortem image?

MANN: A common problem is that pieces of the skull or teeth are often missing. So again, you have to make educated guesses.

In this case, the artist had nothing but a skull to work with. In Case #2, the artist has an eyewitness. But can witnesses always be trusted?

Lincoln Park
Spokane, Washington
November 2, 1996

The Man Who Knew Too Much

A woman is killed in a park, and her husband lives to tell the story. Can a forensic artist unmask the murderer?

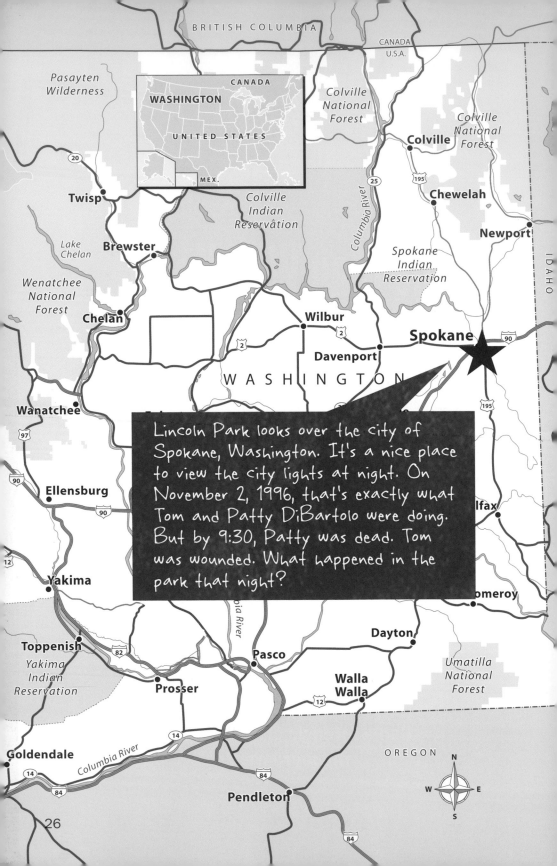

BRITISH COLUMBIA

CANADA
U.S.A.

Pasayten
Wilderness

WASHINGTON

CANADA

UNITED STATES

MEX.

Colville
National
Forest

Colville

Colville
National
Forest

Twisp

Colville
Indian
Reservation

Chewelah

Newport

Lake
Chelan

Brewster

Columbia River

Spokane
Indian
Reservation

IDAHO

Wenatchee
National
Forest

Chelan

Wilbur

Spokane

Davenport

W A S H I N G T O N

Wanatchee

Lincoln Park looks over the city of
Spokane, Washington. It's a nice place
to view the city lights at night. On
November 2, 1996, that's exactly what
Tom and Patty DiBartolo were doing.
But by 9:30, Patty was dead. Tom
was wounded. What happened in the
park that night?

Ellensburg

lfax

Yakima

omeroy

Dayton

Toppenish
Yakima
Indian
Reservation

Prosser

Pasco

Walla
Walla

Umatilla
National
Forest

Goldendale

Columbia River

OREGON

N
W   E
S

Pendleton

Murder in the Park!

**An ex-cop says his wife was killed by a mugger—
and he knows what the killer looks like.**

It was the night of November 2, 1996. A van sped through the streets of Spokane, Washington. The driver, Tom DiBartolo, called 911 on his cell phone. He and his wife, Patty DiBartolo, had been walking in Lincoln Park, he said. An attacker had shot them both. Patty was not doing well.

Patty DiBartolo was murdered one evening in November 1996. She and her husband, Tom DiBartolo, had just been for a walk in the park.

At 9:30 P.M., the van pulled into Sacred Heart Medical Center. Patty was rushed to the emergency room. It was already too late. She had been dead for 30 or 40 minutes. Tom had been shot in the side but was not in serious danger.

Police met Tom DiBartolo at the hospital. To the officers, he was a familiar face. DiBartolo had worked for the Spokane Sheriff's Department for 18 years. He and his wife had five kids. They had been married for 19 years.

DiBartolo told the officers his story. A little before 9 P.M., he said, his pager went off. He and his wife went back to their van. Tom unlocked the passenger door. Two men stepped out of the shadows. One grabbed Patty's gun from the glove box. He fired at

After the shooting, Tom DiBartolo brought his wife here, to the Sacred Heart Medical Center. By the time they arrived, Patty was dead.

least twice. One of the bullets hit Patty DiBartolo in the head.

Tom struggled to get the gun back from the attackers. In the struggle, he was shot in the side. The attackers ran off. Tom pulled his wife into the van and drove off. The hospital was only a few miles away.

The officers asked Tom if he had gotten a good look at the shooter. He said he had. Police decided he should meet with a forensic artist.

Face to Face

The forensic artist meets the witness. And she doesn't like what she hears.

The Spokane police called forensic artist Carrie Stuart Parks. Parks worked for the North Idaho Regional Crime Lab. She agreed to take the case.

Parks met Tom DiBartolo at the Spokane Police Department. The two sat down together in an interview room. Parks started asking questions.

Carrie Stuart Parks is the forensic artist who met with Tom Di Bartolo. Almost immediately, Parks sensed that something was wrong.

Forensic artists create sketches based on the details witnesses give them. Sketches can go through many changes. A witness may ask for features or facial expressions to be changed. This sketch was done by Carrie Stuart Parks for another case.

DiBartolo described the shooter. He told Parks the color of his hair, eyes, and skin. He described the shape of his head, nose, chin, mouth, and cheeks. He remembered the length of his neck and the size of his ears. He even remembered what the man's collar looked like.

Minutes into the interview, Parks knew something was wrong. Like all composite artists, Parks is trained to spot liars.

In this case, a lie was the last thing she expected. Police had said nothing about DiBartolo being a suspect. He was a cop, after all. He had raised five kids with the victim.

Still, Parks had a bad feeling about the interview. The average witness remembers four or five of a criminal's facial features. DiBartolo described every detail of the shooter's face. And he had only seen the man for a few seconds.

Could it be that DiBartolo was lying? Was the real killer sitting across the table from Parks?

THE QUESTION
(?)

Forensic artist Lois Gibson keeps a collection of her sketches. They're right next to the mug shots taken when the suspects are arrested. She has helped to identify more than 700 suspects in 20 years.

The witnesses for this sketch were two (2) twelve (12) year

THE EVIDENCE

Parks decided to test DiBartolo.

He had described the shooter as young, angry, and scared. Parks drew a man who looked calm. DiBartolo said nothing. He accepted the first drawing Parks showed him. Normally, witnesses ask for changes while Parks draws. According to DiBartolo, Parks had gotten it exactly right—on the first try.

That was all Parks needed to know. DiBartolo was lying. She was sure of it.

20 QUESTIONS

How do composite artists know if they should trust a witness's eye?

Most witnesses have no reason to lie. But they can simply be wrong. Try describing someone you've only seen once. Was her hair shoulder-length or shorter? What color were her eyes? Did the cheekbones stand out or not?

It's not easy to remember a person's features. To test a witness's memory, forensic artists ask a series of questions.

1. For how long did you view the criminal? The longer you look at something, the easier it is to remember.

2. What was your point of view? The drawing should be done from the same angle.

3. Was there anything blocking your view? If there was anything blocking the view, that makes an eyewitness less reliable.

4. What was the lighting like? People look different in different types of lighting.

5. How far away were you? The closer the better.

6. Was the criminal moving? Were you moving? Movement can blur the way a person's features look.

7. How long ago did you see the criminal? Memory fades over time.

Busted

The stories don't line up—and Tom DiBartolo is arrested.

Parks spoke to the police. She gave them her composite drawing. But she asked them not to release it to reporters.

Tom DiBartolo was lying, Parks said. She believed he had murdered his wife. Then he'd covered it up by shooting himself in the side.

Police brought Tom DiBartolo back in for questioning. Parts of his story didn't make sense. The hospital was only a few minutes from the park. According to doctors, Patty DiBartolo had been dead for at least a half hour when she arrived. Why did it take her husband so long to get her to the hospital?

Police learned more about DiBartolo's private life. Tom and Patty had been having problems.

Detectives decided they had learned enough. In December they arrested Tom DiBartolo for the murder of his wife. DiBartolo insisted he was innocent. "It's not true, so there's no reason even to **speculate**."

Like Carrie Stuart Parks, Robin Burcell (*above*) is a forensic artist. She is also the author of crime novels. Here, Burcell is looking over some sketches.

Case Closed!

Tom DiBartolo is found guilty of his wife's murder.

Tom DiBartolo went to trial a year after his arrest. By this time, **prosecutors** had more hard evidence. Police had examined the jacket DiBartolo wore the night of the shooting. They found traces of gunpowder in the right pocket. This **residue** matched the type of gunpowder left on his shirt from the gunshot wound. Police also found a glove in the left pocket of the jacket. The glove had no gunpowder residue on it. And the mate to the glove was missing.

Ray Pellegrin is a forensic scientist from Washington State. Here, he is holding Tom DiBartolo's jacket. It had traces of gunpowder in one pocket.

Lawyers argued that DiBartolo killed his wife for the life insurance money. They claimed that he shot his wife with the gloves on. Then he shot himself in the side. He placed the gun in his right jacket pocket. The gun had just been fired, so it left gunpowder residue in his pocket. DiBartolo then dragged his wife's body into the van. On the way to the hospital, he threw the glove and the gun out the window.

Parks added her part of the evidence at the trial. "I couldn't say that Tom lied to me," she remembers. "That was up to the **jury** to decide." Instead she told the jury what witnesses usually remember. Then she described DiBartolo's unusually perfect memory.

The jury got the point. On December 12, 1997, DiBartolo was convicted of first-degree murder. He was sentenced to 26 years in prison for killing his wife.

Parks still remembers her encounter with DiBartolo well. "It was one of the most disturbing composites I'd ever done," she says. "I didn't expect a police officer, husband, and father to be a killer." 24/7

Tom DiBartolo, a former sheriff's deputy, was found guilty of murdering his wife on December 12, 1997.

Forensic Artist Carrie Stuart Parks has her own built-in lie detector.

24/7: Do you often suspect a witness is lying?

PARKS: Cops are suspicious of *everyone*. Because of their jobs, they are exposed to the most rotten side of people. But I take the middle ground: I test people.

24/7: What do you ask witnesses in order to test them?

PARKS: I'd tell you but I'd have to kill you. [*She laughs.*] Actually, there are a number of things I look for. An important one is **consistency** of the choices the witness makes when describing facial features. I compare their answers to what I would expect them to say based on the information I have been given by police.

24/7: What are some of the trigger words that make you suspicious?

PARKS: "You know" is a trigger when the witness has not used those words elsewhere. Some other trigger words are: "Honestly," as in "I honestly don't know." Or "swear," as in "I swear I'm telling the truth." "Never," is another one, as in "I never lie." A lot of denials also trigger my "lie detector." For example, a witness may say, "No, no, no, I didn't see anyone, no."

[Forensic Fact]
Research has shown that people are able to better recognize and describe people who are the same race as they are.

In this case, a suspicious forensic artist helped solve a murder. In the next case, can another artist help a man track down his missing daughter?

Washington, D.C.
August 4, 1993

The Case of the Missing Girl

A four-year-old girl is kidnapped
by her mother. Thirteen years
later, police are still searching for
her. But what does the girl—now
17 years old—look like?

Girl Kidnapped

Marilyn Byrd and her mother have disappeared without a trace.

On August 4, 1993, Carl Dodd went to visit his daughter. Four-year-old Marilyn lived with her mother, Mary Jane Byrd, and her grandmother in Washington, D.C. Dodd and Byrd had broken up years before.

On that August day in 1993, Dodd arrived to pick up Marilyn. But no one was home. Mary Jane Byrd and Marilyn had vanished.

Dodd called the police. But weeks passed, and they made no progress.

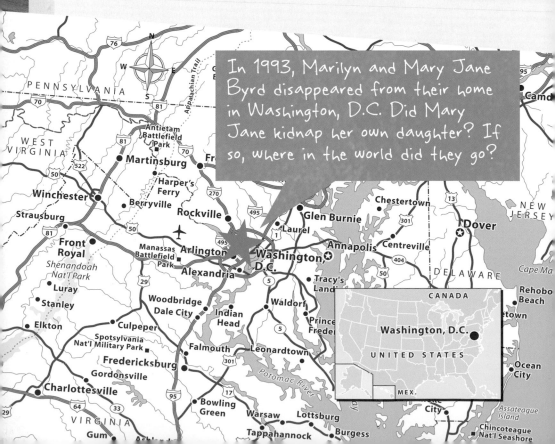

In 1993, Marilyn and Mary Jane Byrd disappeared from their home in Washington, D.C. Did Mary Jane kidnap her own daughter? If so, where in the world did they go?

Carl Dodd learned that there was little the police could do to help him find his daughter.

Dodd wanted custody of his daughter. So he went to family court. Several months later, the court ruled in his favor. Dodd now had the right to take care of his daughter. But he would have to find her first.

Looking for Marilyn

Dodd refuses to give up the search. But as the years go by, how will he know what his daughter looks like?

Several years went by. Carl Dodd spent thousands of dollars searching for Marilyn. He hired detectives and lawyers.

Dodd and his wife, Paula, often drove by Byrd's home in Washington, D.C. The couple would wait and watch. They looked for signs of Marilyn. But they found nothing.

Eventually, Detective Rick Adams was assigned to the case. He asked for help from the National Center for Missing and Exploited Children (NCMEC). The NCMEC was created in the 1980s to help

Marilyn was abducted when she was four. This photo was taken just before the abduction.

The National Center for Missing and Exploited Children (NCMEC) was founded in 1984 to help protect and find missing children.

protect missing and abused children. In **abduction** cases, the NCMEC often sends out photos of missing children.

An abduction is a kidnapping.

The NCMEC wanted to help find Marilyn. By this time, though, no one knew what she looked like. The NCMEC called in forensic artist Glenn Miller.

Miller directs the group's Forensic Services Unit. He spent 23 years as a police officer before joining NCMEC. He'd been trained by the **FBI** in forensic art.

Miller's job was to create an **age-progression** image of Marilyn. He needed to predict how the years had changed the way Marilyn looked.

Miller started by collecting evidence. Dodd gave him photos of Marilyn at age four.

Marilyn's case was difficult. Miller had very little personal information. But he had years of experience and research to work with. Forensic artists are trained to understand how the human face ages. And most faces age in predictable ways. When children grow up, their faces get longer. The section below the eyes grows longer than the section above the eyes. The features begin to stick out more.

Miller used all of this data to create the new image of Marilyn. First, he scanned one of the four-year-old pictures into the computer. He then used special software to carefully change the image.

The new image showed a smiling Marilyn with straight black hair and bangs. The NCMEC printed posters. They ran the photo on their Web site.

Adams and Dodd were now even more determined to find Marilyn. The detective told Dodd, "I'm not going to retire until I find your child."

SHANNON SHERRILL

Non-Family Abduction
Age Progressed

DOB: Aug 12, 1980
Missing: Oct 5, 1986
Age Now: 22
Sex: Female
Race: White
Hair: Brown
Eyes: Blue
Height: 3'0" (91 cm)
Weight: 30 lbs (14 kg)
Missing From:
THORNTOWN
IN
United States

Shannon's photo is shown age-progressed to 19 years. She was last seen at 1:30 p.m. playing in her yard with several other children wearing a white dress with blue trim. She has a 4 inch scar on her abdomen, pierced ears, and is extremely shy.

MISSING & EXPLOITED CHILDREN

ANYONE HAVING INFORMATION SHOULD CONTACT
National Center for Missing & Exploited Children
1-800-843-5678 (1-800-THE-LOST)

Thorntown Police Department (Indiana) - Missing Persons Unit - 1-317-436-7677 OR Your Lo...

A Breakthrough
Officials follow new leads to Marilyn.

Dodd and Adams suffered through several more years of disappointment. Then, in December 2005, they found new hope. The federal government began a push to track down parents accused of kidnapping their kids. The FBI and the U.S. Marshals started

Here is an example of age-progression photos. These photos appeared on the NCMEC Web site. On the left is Shannon Sherrill, age six. The photo to the right shows how she might have looked in July 2003, as a 19-year-old woman.

Above: Reporters surrounded the home where Marilyn Byrd was found in April 2006. *Above right:* To protect Marilyn's privacy, her head was covered with a coat as she left her mother's house. She is walking with a U.S. marshal.

to hunt for Marilyn Byrd. At this point, she had been missing for almost 13 years. Her case was one of the oldest of its kind.

The marshals checked out every possible lead in the case. Several people told them that Mary Jane might be in Wilmington, Delaware. The marshals asked Glenn Miller to update his image of Marilyn. They went to Wilmington with the new picture.

The picture soon got them new leads. At 7:30 A.M. on April 12, 2006, they entered a gray house. Upstairs, they found a woman and a teenage girl. The girl looked a lot like the face in Glenn Miller's image.

It was Mary Jane and Marilyn Byrd. The marshals arrested Mary Jane Byrd for kidnapping her daughter. It was Marilyn Byrd's 17th birthday.

On April 17, 2006, Carl Dodd made a trip to Wilmington to see Marilyn. He had not seen her since she was four years old. When Dodd saw Marilyn, he recognized her right away. She had his lips and nose.

Since then, the father, mother, and daughter have all faced many changes.

Marilyn lives with her mother. But she's getting to know her father. And she started counseling to deal with everything.

Mary Jane Byrd faces a trial for abduction. And Carl Dodd sent Marilyn a cell phone. They've been speaking once or twice a week. For Carl, that's a step in the right direction. 24/7

FAST-FORWARD
How does the human face change over time?

Forensic artists like Glenn Miller need to imagine how a person might age. They dig up as many clues as they can. Here are some of them.

Photos: An artist looks for pictures taken at different angles. Photos of family members help, too. People often look like their relatives.

Ancestry/Ethnicity: Ethnic background can affect how people age. Over time, people with dark skin are damaged less by the sun than people with fair skin.

Medical history: Plastic surgery, weight changes, and dental work make a difference. Bad eyesight might cause people to start to wear glasses.

Lifestyle information: Someone who smokes, drinks heavily, takes drugs, or spends a lot of time in the sun may look older than someone who doesn't.

Facial changes: As time goes on, the face goes through predictable changes.

When kids grow up, their faces get longer. Foreheads look flatter. Jaws become more defined. Noses get longer, and eyes become less rounded.

As adults age, their jaws become less defined. The skin wrinkles. In the 20s, lines appear between the eyes and the eyebrows. In the 30s, the lines show up between the sides of the nose and the mouth. In the 40s, the neck gets wrinkled.

Forensic artist Glenn Miller speaks for kids who can't speak for themselves.

24/7: Why is age progression so important in missing child cases?

MILLER: As time goes by, original pictures of a child are of no value. Children change so much in a short time. Law enforcement needs a tool to help them continue to look for the child.

Age-progression images often give families new hope. To date, we've had about 680 children recovered when an age progression has been done. In some cases, the image is the only reason the child is found.

24/7: How did you feel when Marilyn was finally found?

MILLER: I felt good about it! The first thing I wanted was a **recovery picture**. When I saw it, I was very happy with the resemblance. It's important for us to get a recovery picture so we can see where we went wrong and right.

24/7: What's the secret to creating good age-progression images?

MILLER: The artist can't put too many of his own ideas into the way a child should look. It's only okay to guess when it comes to things like hair and clothes. But it's important to get things like the eyes, nose, and mouth right. These parts must be completely accurate for the image to be useful.

A recovery picture is a photo of a person when he or she has been found.

FORENSIC
DOWNLOAD

Here's even more amazing stuff about forensic art for you to picture.

1881 Train Murderer Busted

A murderer kills a wealthy man on a train outside London. He jumps off the train and escapes. Witnesses describe the killer to an artist. A newspaper prints the composite drawing. And the picture leads police right to murderer Percy Lefroy Mapleton.

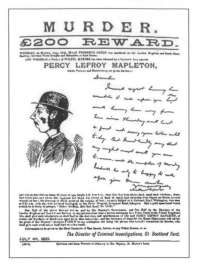

Key Dates in

1935 Identifying the Dead

Two skulls are found in Scotland. Police think one may belong to a missing woman named Isabella Ruxton *(below left)*. They compare a photo of Ruxton to a photo of one of the skulls. According to police, the two photos match. The method is not scientific. But it helps lead to postmortem imaging.

1950s Build a Face

Forensic artists develop a tool for doing composite drawings. The first "Identi-KIT" comes with sheets called "foils." The foils show different types of facial features. Witnesses can pick foils that match the criminal they've seen. The artist puts the foils together to form a face. The witness asks for changes until the image looks exactly right.

1967 Made from Clay

Medical artist Betty Gatliff makes a clay model of a head from a skull. A photo of the model is published. A man recognizes it as his son, Rudy Findley. Gatliff is now known as the pioneer of 3-D facial reconstructions.

1984 FBI Art School

The FBI Academy holds its first artist's training program in Quantico, Virginia. The program is run by Horace Heafner. Heafner trained Glenn Miller, the forensic artist in Case #3.

Forensic Art

How did people figure out that art could help solve mysteries? It all started with a murder.

1984 NCMEC Is Formed

The National Center for Missing and Exploited Children (NCMEC) is created. The group uses forensic art to help find missing children. In 2006, they helped find Marilyn Byrd, who had been kidnapped 13 years earlier. Shown here is John Walsh, host of *America's Most Wanted* and co-founder of NCMEC.

See Case #3: The Case of the Missing Girl.

In the News

Read about it!
Forensic art is
front-page news.

Forensic Artists Go High-Tech

MONTGOMERY COUNTY, MD—November 17, 2005

In the future, forensic artists may not need to be good at art. According to the *Washington Post*, police in Montgomery County are using computers to draw composite images. Forensic artists still interview witnesses directly. The witnesses describe a suspect, feature by feature.

Then the artist creates a portrait using computer-generated noses, mouths, hats, and other details. The finished face can be adjusted with a click of a mouse.

Artists who use the program say it works well. But Detective Deborah Haba said it has some drawbacks. "In my **database**, the headwear looks like it's from the 1970s," she said. "I had to create my own do-rags because we don't have do-rags in the database."

Detective Gary Irwin still won't put down his pencil. "Your sketch is only as good as your artist," he says.

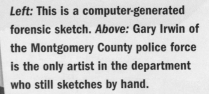

Left: This is a computer-generated forensic sketch. *Above:* Gary Irwin of the Montgomery County police force is the only artist in the department who still sketches by hand.

46

New Technology Compares Art and Life

FLORENCE, ITALY—May 2005

Investigators don't just use forensic art to solve crimes. Some use it to study art.

Recently, some investigators tried to answer this question: Did famous artists make their wealthy subjects look better than real life? According to Italian researchers, the answer is yes. A new article in the *Journal of Forensic Sciences* reports their discovery.

The scientists were working with a 16th-century skeleton. They weren't sure whom it belonged to. So they took digital photos of the skull.

The researchers also photographed a portrait of an Italian woman named Eleonora Gonzaga della Rovere. The portrait was done by the painter Titian. The researchers then laid the photos of the skull over the photos of the painting. They matched, except for one detail. Titian made the duchess's nose longer. Long noses were a sign of beauty in 16th-century Italy.

In her day, she was a beauty. This is a painting of Eleonora Gonzaga della Rovere. Did the artist really paint her nose longer to make her seem more glamorous?

Face to Face

Have a look at the tools, equipment, forms, and other gadgets used by a forensic artist.

pencils and paper Forensic artists who draw their images use pencils and paper. Pencils can be made of lead, graphite, or charcoal. Paper should be thick so it won't tear if the artist has to erase.

blending tools The lines on forensic art drawings usually need to be blended, or smudged a little bit. To blend, artists often use the tip of their finger. Now that's a cheap art tool!

skull and tissue markers Postmortem reconstruction artists have special tools. Often they reconstruct faces from skulls. They attach tissue markers to a skull. The markers show where the lines and curves of the face once were.

plaster or clay Some forensic artists make plaster or clay sculptures instead of drawing. They study a skull and then make a model of the head. Then they add lips, eyes, a nose, ears, and other features.

computer software Forensic artists also use computers. The newest art software creates very realistic images of people. Artists can put together a face from a huge selection of features. They can change details with the click of a mouse.

FORMS

Forensic artists use charts like this one to help them figure out how a person's face might look. The charts show average facial measurements for different ethnic groups. The measurements vary for men and women and for people of different weights. The charts tell artists how much tissue belongs at 21 different points on the skull. Artists use the measurements to place tissue markers at these points. The points are called **anthropological landmarks**. They include the brows, cheeks, chin, and other features.

Table 11.2 Tissue Thicknesses (in millimeters) of American Caucasoids (European-derived) by Rhine and Moore[a]

Measurement	Slender Male (3)	Slender Female (3)	Normal Male (37)	Normal Female (19)	Obese Male (8)	Obese Female (3)
Midline						
1. Supraglabella	2.25	2.50	4.25	3.50	5.50	4.25
2. Glabella	2.50	4.00	5.25	4.75	7.50	7.50
3. Nasion	4.25	5.25	6.50	5.50	7.50	7.00
4. End of nasals	2.50	2.25	3.00	2.75	3.50	4.25
5. Mid-philtrum	6.25	5.00	10.00	8.50	11.00	9.00
6. Upper lip margin	9.75[b]	6.25	9.75	9.00	11.00	11.00
7. Lower lip margin	9.50[b]	8.50	11.00	10.00	12.75	12.25
8. Chin–lip fold	8.75	9.25	10.75	9.50	12.25	13.75
9. Mental eminence	7.00	8.50	11.25	10.00	14.00	14.25
10. Beneath chin	4.50	3.75	7.25	5.75	10.75	9.00

11. Frontal eminence	6.
12. Supraorbital	2.2
13. Suborbital	8.5(
14. Inferior malar	5.00
15. Lateral orbit	3.00
16. Zygomatic arch, halfway	4.25
17. Supraglenoid	4.50
18. Gonion	12.00
19. Supra M²	12.00
20. Occlusal line	10.00
21. Sub M₂	

Adapted from Rhine and Moore, 1982; revi-
-d C. Elliot Moore II, Ph.D., through the co-
-dical Investigator, State of New Mexico.
... Stanley Rhine, Ph.D.
-- .. Weston, M.D., Office of the

3 Artists; 1 Mummy

Three forensic teams were given the same models of King Tut. They were told to re-create the king's face. How would their art compare?

Ever wonder what a 3,000-year-old Egyptian mummy looked like—when he was alive? That's exactly the question scientists asked in 2005. They turned to forensic artists to find the answer.

That January, scientists dug up the remains of the famous teenage pharaoh, King Tut. Tut's remains were placed in a CT scanner. A CT scan is a kind of x-ray. It shows a three-dimensional view of the body. The scan produced 1,700 images. From the images, scientists created a model of Tut's skull.

The scientists then put together three teams of artists and scientists. The teams used the images and the skull to reconstruct King Tut's face. What did they come up with? See for yourself.

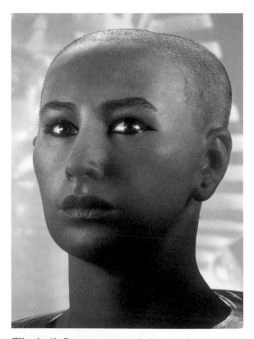

THE FRENCH TEAM

The French team was told all the details. They knew they had scans and a skull model from the famous King Tut. They studied the evidence. They confirmed that the remains were from a male between the ages of 18 and 20. Their sculptor, Elisabeth Daynes, created this likeness.

Elisabeth Daynes created this sculpture for the French team.

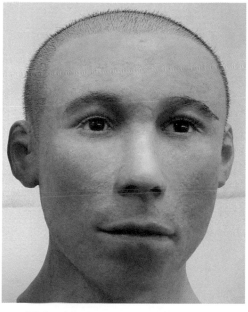

Michael Anderson sculpted this figure for the U.S. team.

THE U.S. TEAM

The U.S. team was given the same scans and skull model. But they were not told who they belonged to. Still, the U.S. team also concluded that the person was an 18- or 19-year-old male. They thought he was from North Africa. Their sculptor, Michael Anderson, made this likeness.

THE EGYPTIAN TEAM

Like the French team, the Egyptians knew the identity of their subject. They created a computer-generated image of the king. The features were partly based on ancient portraits of Tut.

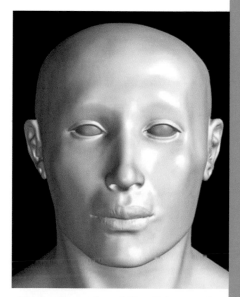

Here's the version of King Tut created by the Egyptian team.

What did the experiment show? The three sculptures look a lot alike. That proves that the forensic techniques work!

HELP WANTED:
Forensic Artist

Can you picture yourself as a forensic artist? Here's more information about the field.

Joy Mann is a forensic artist in Wheaton, IL.

Q&A: JOY MANN

24/7: How did you become interested in forensic art?

MANN: I was always an artist. I began to ask about age progression for missing children about 12 years ago. A friend in law enforcement introduced me to forensic art, and I became hooked!

24/7: Did you always know that you wanted to do this as a career?

MANN: No. I was pursuing law school and got detoured.

24/7: What's the most difficult part of your job?

MANN: There are two things: Seeing people hurt or grieving is hard. It's also tough to get law enforcement officials to understand what a difference a good forensic artist can make.

24/7: What part of your job do you enjoy the most?

MANN: Seeing the joy that my work can bring people. This includes finding and convicting a suspect. It also means providing help to a family with age-progression drawings.

24/7: What advice would you give teens who are interested in forensic art?

MANN: Work on two basic skills and develop them. 1) Develop your artistic skills. Look at, draw, and study the human face and anatomy. 2) Develop your people skills. Listen, be patient, and learn to communicate.

24/7: Anything else you'd like to add?

MANN: Forensic art is not a "big money" occupation. But it is one of the most satisfying and meaningful fields one can encounter.

THE STATS

DAY JOB
Many forensic artists work in law enforcement. They do forensic art as needed. They are investigators, clerks, and patrol officers.

Some forensic artists also have their own businesses. They are used as independent consultants by law enforcement agencies, such as the police and the FBI.

MONEY
Forensic artists who are also working police officers can make anywhere from $20,000 to $60,000 a year. Generally, forensic artists who work in larger cities make more than those in small towns.

EDUCATION
Certification by the International Association for Identification (IAI) or the FBI. This requires:
▶ 80 hours of education in the field of composite art from an approved school. See the IAI Web site.
▶ at least one year full-time experience in forensic art and 25 completed hand-drawn composites
▶ 2 successful composite drawings

53

DO YOU HAVE WHAT IT TAKES?

Take this totally unscientific quiz to find out if forensic art might be a good career for you.

1 **Do you like to solve complicated puzzles?**
   a) Yes. I'm very patient and keep working until I finish.
   b) If I'm in a certain mood, I like to do a puzzle.
   c) Puzzles drive me crazy.

2 **Are you interested in computers?**
   a) Yes, I'm always trying to learn new software.
   b) It's a good tool.
   c) I just use my computer to check my e-mail.

3 **Are you good with people?**
   a) I can talk to anyone.
   b) I can hold my own when I have to.
   c) I dislike having to talk to anyone but my cat.

4 **Can you draw?**
   a) Yes. I've always been able to draw well.
   b) I can draw some things well.
   c) No. I'm not really an artist.

5 **Would you get freaked out if you had to work with a dead person?**
   a) I don't think so. I think I could just concentrate on the problem I'm trying to solve.
   b) I'm not really sure. But I'm willing to give it a try.
   c) I feel sick just thinking about that question.

YOUR SCORE

Give yourself 3 points for every "a" you chose.
Give yourself 2 points for every "b" you chose.
Give yourself 1 point for every "c" you chose.

If you got **13–15 points**, you'd probably be a good forensic artist.

If you got **10–12 points**, you might be a good forensic artist.

If you got **5–9 points**, you might want to look at another career!

54

HOW TO GET STARTED...NOW!

It's never too early to start working toward your goals.

GET AN EDUCATION

▶ Focus on your computer and art classes. Science is also important, especially biology.

▶ Start thinking about college. Look for schools with good art and science programs. It's not essential, but it wouldn't hurt to find a college with forensic science classes.

▶ Read the newspaper.

▶ Keep up with what's going on in your community.

▶ Read anything you can find about forensic art. See the books and Web sites in the Resources section on pages 56–58.

▶ Graduate from high school!

NETWORK!

▶ Find out about forensic groups in your area.

▶ See if you can find a forensic artist who might be willing to give you advice.

▶ Try a Web search. Some forensic artists have Web sites.

GET AN INTERNSHIP

▶ Look for an internship with a local law enforcement agency.

▶ Look for an internship with a forensic artist.

LEARN ABOUT OTHER JOBS IN THE FIELD

There are lots of jobs in crime-solving that require an eye for detail.

▶ Police officer
▶ Crime scene analyst
▶ Crime scene technician
▶ Forensic technician
▶ Detective
▶ Criminalist
▶ Crime lab supervisor

55

Resources

Looking for more information about forensic art? Here are some resources you don't want to miss!

PROFESSIONAL ORGANIZATIONS

American Academy of Forensic Sciences (AAFS)
www.aafs.org
410 North 21st Street
Colorado Springs, CO 80904-2798
PHONE: 719-636-1100

The AAFS is a professional society dedicated to the application of science to the law. It promotes education and accuracy in the forensic sciences.

International Association for Identification (IAI)
www.theiai.org
2535 Pilot Knob Road, Suite 117
Mendota Heights, MN 55120-1120
PHONE: 651-681-8566
FAX: 651-681-8443

The IAI is the oldest and largest forensic organization in the world. It is a forum where forensic specialists worldwide can interact. Its goal is training and research to ensure all specialists maintain the highest levels of integrity and professionalism.

Canadian Society of Forensic Science (CSFS)
www.csfs.ca
P.O. Box 37040
3332 McCarthy Road
Ottawa, Ontario
Canada K1V 0W0
PHONE: 613-738-0001
EMAIL: csfs@bellnet.ca

The CSFS is a nonprofit professional organization that tries to maintain professional standards and promote the study and enhance the stature of forensic science. Membership in the society is open internationally to professionals with an active interest in the forensic sciences. It is organized into sections representing diverse areas of forensic examination: Anthropology, Medical, Odontology, Biology, Chemistry, Documents, Engineering, and Toxicology.

Centre of Forensic Sciences (CFS)

www.mpss.jus.gov.on.ca/english/
pub_safety/centre_forensic/about/
intro.html

Ministry of Community Safety
and Correctional Services
18th Floor
25 Grosvenor Street
Toronto, Ontario
M7A IY6

PHONE: 416-326-5010

The CFS is one of the most extensive forensic science facilities in North America. The two laboratories conduct scientific investigations in cases involving injury or death in unusual circumstances and in crimes against persons or property.

WEB SITES

Court TV's Crime Library
www.crimelibrary.com/criminal_
mind/forensics/art/2.html
This section of the site focuses on forensic artists and what they do.

Discovery Channel
http://dsc.discovery.com/
fansites/onthecase/qa/qa_01.html
Here is an interview with forensic artist Karen Taylor.

Forensic Faces Institute
www.forensicart.org
This site provides information about the work of forensic artists.

Forensic Magazine
www.forensicmag.com
This site is for a leading publication about forensic science.

Karen T. Taylor Facial Images
www.karenttaylor.com/FORENSIC
home.html
This is the Web site of Karen Taylor, a noted forensic artist.

Mannhunters
www.mannhunters.com
This is the Web site for contributor Joy Mann.

National Center for Missing and Exploited Children
www.missingkids.com
Visit this site to learn more about this group and its work.

National Geographic: Unraveling the Mysteries of King Tutankhamun
http://magma.nationalgeographic.
com/ngm/tut/mysteries/
forensics.html
This site offers more information about the study of King Tut.

Stuart Parks Forensic Associates
www.stuartparks.com
This is the Web site for contributor Carrie Stuart Parks.

COURSES AND SPECIALIZED PROGRAMS

There are very few colleges or universities that offer programs specifically in forensic art. But there are a number of different places where you can take courses to become certified. Here are two Web sites to check out.

FBI Laboratory Specialized Training Program:
www.fbi.gov/hq/lab/fsc/backissu/oct2005/communications/2005_10_communications02.htm

International Association for Identification Forensic Artist Certification:
www.theiai.org/certifications/artist/index.php

PROFESSIONAL BOOKS

Fisher, Barry A. J. *Techniques of Crime Scene Investigation, 7th ed.* Boca Raton, Fla.: CRC Press, 2003.

Genge, Ngaire, E. *The Forensic Casebook: The Science of Crime Scene Investigation.* New York: Ballantine, 2002.

Taylor, Karen T. *Forensic Art and Illustration.* Boca Raton, Fla.: CRC Press, 2000.

BOOKS FOR KIDS ABOUT FORENSIC SCIENCE

Camenson, Blythe. *Opportunities in Forensic Science Careers.* New York; McGraw-Hill, 2001.

Ferllini, Roxana. *Silent Witness: How Forensic Anthropology Is Used to Solve the World's Toughest Crimes.* Ontario: Firefly Books, 2002.

Platt, Richard. *Ultimate Guide to Forensic Science.* New York: DK Publishing, 2003.

Rainis, Kenneth G. *Crime-Solving Science Projects: Forensic Science Experiments.* Berkeley Heights, N.J.: Enslow Publishing, 2000.

Walker, Pam, and Elaine Wood. *Crime Scene Investigations: Real-Life Science Labs for Grades 6–12.* New York: Jossey-Bass, 1998.

A

abduction (ab-DUKT-shun) *noun* the illegal capture and taking of someone

age progession (ayj pruh-GRESH-un) *noun* the process of determining what someone will look like over time

anthropological landmarks (an-thruh-puh-LOJ-uh-kul land-marks) *noun* the 21 points on the skull where there are various amounts of tissue. There are charts that show forensic artists how much tissue are generally on these anthoropolic landmarks, depending on the victim's gender, age, and ethnicity.

autopsy (AH-top-see) *noun* a medical exam done on a dead body to figure out the cause of death

C

composite image (kuhm-POZ-it IH-muj) *noun* a type of forensic art in which a person is drawn based on descriptions of the different parts of the human face

consistency (kun-SIS-tun-see) *noun* the state of all the parts of something being alike or agreeing with one another

corpse (korps) *noun* a dead human body

cranium (KRAY-nee-um) *noun* the part of the skull that protects the brain

D

database (DAY-tuh-bayss) *noun* a lot of information organized on a computer

DNA (DEE-en-ay) *noun* a chemical found in almost every cell of your body. It's a blueprint for the way you look and function.

E

ethnic background (ETH-nik BAK-grownd) *noun* information about a person's race

evidence (EV-uh-duhnss) *noun* information and facts that help you prove something

expert (EX-purt) *noun* someone who knows a lot about a certain subject. For a list of forensic experts, see page 12.

Dictionary

F

FBI (ef-BEE-eye) *noun* a U.S. government agency that investigates major crimes. It's short for *Federal Bureau of Investigation*.

features (FEE-churz) *noun* the parts that make up the human face

forensic (fuh-REN-sik) *adjective* describing a science that relates to the law and solving crimes

forensic art (fuh-REN-sik art) *noun* any art that helps capture a criminal or that finds a criminal guilty. Forensic art can also help identify unknown dead bodies. People who create forensic art are called forensic artists.

H

hit (hit) *noun* a successful identification

I

identify (eye-DEN-tuh-fye) *verb* to figure out who someone is

J

Jane Doe (jayn doh) *noun* an unidentified female body

John Doe (jon doh) *noun* an unidentified male body

jury (JU-ree) *noun* a group of people who listen to a court case and decide if someone is guilty or innocent

M

mandible (MAN-duh-bull) *noun* the lower jawbone

N

nasal bone (NAY-zul bone) *noun* the bridge of the nose

P

postmortem (pohst-MORE-tuhm) *adjective* after death

postmortem identification image (pohst-MORE-tuhm eye-den-tuh-fih-KAY-shun IH-muj) *noun* a type of forensic art in which a drawing or sculpture of a dead person is made to show what the person looked like

prosecutor (PROSS-uh-kyoo-tur) *noun* a lawyer who represents the government in criminal trials

R

reconstruct (REE-khun-strukt) *verb* to build again

reconstruction (REE-khun-strukt-shun) *noun* something that has been rebuilt

recovery picture (rI-KUHV-ur-ee PIK-chur) *noun* a photo taken when a missing person is found. Forensic artists compare these with their sketches to see how accurate they were.

remains (ri-MAYNZ) *noun* what is left of a body after someone has died

residue (REZ-uh-doo) *noun* anything that is left after the main part of something is taken away. Gunshot residue is evidence left after a gun is fired.

S

sculpture (SKUHLP-chur) *noun* a piece of art carved or shaped out of stone, metal, marble, clay, or some similar material

skull (skuhl) *noun* the bony frame of the head

space alien (spayss ay-LEE-uhn) *noun* an odd-looking composite drawing

speculate (SPEK-yuh-late) *verb* to wonder or guess about something without having all the facts

suspect (SUHS-pekt) *noun* a person law enforcement officials think might be guilty of a crime

T

tissue markers (TISH-oo MAR-kurz) *noun* small plastic pieces glued directly to a skull that act as a guide to the shape and curves of the face. The length of each marker is determined by things like race, gender, and weight.

V

victim (VIK-tum) *noun* a person who is injured, killed, or mistreated

W

witness (WIT-niss) *noun* a person who is present during a crime, sees it, or has personal knowledge of it. An eyewitness saw a crime take place and can describe it.

Z

zygomatic bone (ZYE-guh-mah-tik bone) *noun* the cheekbone

Index

Author's Note

If you Google the term "forensic art," you'll get more than 40,000 results! There are a whole lot of other people besides you who think forensic art is cool.

But beware: When reading or writing about real-life stuff, be sure to check your facts! In the process of writing this book, I found that books, Web sites, and articles didn't always agree with each other. One would have a piece of information that I thought was interesting or useful. But when I compared it to another source, sometimes the information was slightly different.

To be certain something is a fact, use many sources. And more important, use *trustworthy* sources. Books and articles by the top experts or well-known news writers are a safe bet.

Be careful about trusting the Internet too much. All Internet sites are not created equal, and some aren't even true! Anyone can post information on the Web. It doesn't mean that it is all well-researched or even true. Check out the Resources section of this book for some of the most helpful sites and books. They'll give you the real lowdown on forensic art.

In researching this book, I had the pleasure of talking with several forensic artists. They were all generous enough to share their experiences with me. After hearing about the cases they work on, I realized just how tough the job of a forensic artist really is. They have to deal with crime, death, and suffering victims all the time. Forensic artists are compassionate people who are truly dedicated to their careers. I hope this book inspires you to think about becoming one!

ACKNOWLEDGEMENTS

I would like to thank all of the forensic artists who contributed to this book. Their time, effort, and expertise were invaluable to its creation. I would also like to thank Kate Waters, Suzanne Harper, Jennifer Wilson, Elizabeth Ward, and Katie Marsico for their support.

CREDITS

Contributing forensic artists:
Joy Mann
Carrie Stuart Parks
Glenn Miller

CONTENT ADVISER: Robin Burcell, forensic artist and author of *Cold Case* and *Deadly Legacy*